YOU AS POETRY

. . .

RÖSE
HUNTER

You As Poetry

•••

ROSE HUNTER

tP
Texture Press
2013

cover based on a photo by the author
cover design by Arlene Ang

published in the United States by Texture Press
1108 Westbrooke Terrace Norman, OK 73072
phone: 405-314-7730
email: texturepress@beyondutopia.com

for ordering information visit the Texture Press website
at www.texturepress.org

ISBN-13: 978-0615877358
ISBN-10: 0615877354

This is a revised edition based on *You As Poems,* 2012.

My most appreciative thank yous to Sherry O'Keefe,
John Riley, and Valerie Fox for their help in editing the
manuscript.

I.

You As International Transfer Lounge   9
You As Insulated Travel Mug   10
You As Los Angeles   11
You As Bosc   12
You As The Cream Cheese, The Aquarium,
         & The Cummerbund   14
You As Intersection   15
You As Whole Foods Box Salad   16

II.

You As Invitation   19
You As Hands   20
You As The Full Catastrophe   21
You As Invasive Exotic   22
You As Sharp Object   24
You As Wreath   25
You As Teeth   26
You As Bathroom Essential   27
You As Crop Staple   28
You As Apples   29
You As Barn Owl   30
You As Weight   31
You As The Rooster   32
You As Cockfight   33
You As Bottle   37

III.

You As Feral Cat   41
You As The Kitten   42
You As Small Space   43
You As Paper Cup   44
You As Canyon   45
You As The Mango   46

You As Squirrel   47
You As White Rabbit   48

IV.

You As Sea Urchin   51
You As Snake   52
You As Me In The Mirror   53
You As Francis Bacon, *Figure With Meat*   54
You As Drag   55
You As More Red   56
You As Levels   57
You As Slots-A-Fun   58
You As Tunnel   59
You As White Wall   60
You As Cold Turkey   61
You As Yellow & Blue   62
You As Corpse   63
You As Puppy Killer   64

V.

You As The Sun   67
You As Botanical Gardens   68
You As The Toad   71
You As Sound   72
You As *Pied-à-terre*   73
You As *Salsa Casera*   74

VI.

You As Leaves   77
You As Fierce Inhabitant Of Brackish Water   78
You As Green Lagoon   79

Acknowledgements   80

I.

You As International Transfer Lounge

where we are to wait, and after
we can tell you nothing except to wait
and like I said about one of your shirts:

now that's announcing: *I'm a shirt.* That one
blue not red, hibiscus but things blur into
twenty-four hours with my bag as a pillow
and nothing to do or be. Drifting
fishing poles, popsicle tongues
and a three ball knitting wool parade

with fields of swaddled humpbacks
and beyond the fall glass
lights on the runway like butter like
on the stairs waiting for you
the alley a waterfall: cascade

you wouldn't even take my hand.
But I had plans for when I got you inside.
I was prepared to clean your pants.
But then you started the dts.

You As Insulated Travel Mug

with stippled belt which is where

it's most natural to grasp you
off a morning, that house in LA

it was cold with holes in the walls
and I thought how, your doors always open

(in one sense); our blood
was not the same stuff and if

I handed you a coffee it was
too hot too; from the frying pan into

the fire you said, and how I shrugged and
here, you are grey as your morning tremor:

vacuum insulated sixteen ounce
stainless steel, autoseal, *Contigo*.

You As Los Angeles

Where you come from and I can't help it
of course I know you have walked along
this street, for example

(and even in Rite Aid
T-shirts maps cigarettes Christmas
decorations CDs soap, laundry
clothes pegs booze, trust me, I said
this is not what's in a "drugstore"
in every country)

(and when I see you in Vallarta
I saw Karl! and you say *in a city
of? twelve million?* All bear
pancake and flapjack & how I liked
to flummox you, but no)
he met me at the airport
but that's another story.

You As Bosc

Karl and Eddie are on the porch
under a haze like gauze
this, my temporary home so

what's real is the way Karl
is sitting, facing Wilcox. Eddie's
got Lexington. Scot has the drift

bird bath and mossy path up to the step
easel and roach, banana skin paint tubes
and mosaiced ice cream containers
while upstairs, Gabi

You shoot me in the leg!
You don't respect
where I'm coming from
you shoot me in the leg!

and the illegitimate
brother of Christian Brando
Eddie says, *or so people think*
and there's no convincing them

that when I say "ghostwriter"
what does it mean to you?
and how many people hiding in Mexico

or homeless at Hollywood and Highland
Scot says, like he bought a T-shirt or a coffee
it was both easy and difficult.

Of all those lost souls he
was the most like you.
The door to his cellar
match drum spark beat

and the smell of pears, bosc
because they smell of dusk
and all that could have happened
one month to the day.

You As The Cream Cheese, The Aquarium & The Cummerbund

I swear the velodrome dip
and flourish, I swear the kitchen plug
sinkhole, opposite the Johnny Rockets

& next to the aquarium. I swear
there are no murals of you, in your Sunday best
& I can't swear I never told you but
only when behind the glass
& if you were here we could talk about

all the people who've died.

You As Intersection

cigarettes lighters knives pipes gifts
ATM Natural American
Spirit Häagen Dazs Maverick
Newport H & K Marlboro
Wrangler Customer Parking
Only Thai Food Holidays Discounts
Fat Sushi Wok 'n Roll Chinese
Philly Steak Depot Hair + Nails By Jorge
Panaderia y Pupuseria, La Guanaquita
and the woman launching out

pulls at her jacket like after a difficult
doctor's appointment or maybe
dental, in which she was told she needed
something expensive (painful in that way)
like a root canal, heads into Yoshinoya
miso soup: made from dashi, made from kelp.

You As Whole Foods Box Salad

& I wanted nothing less than the
world so I filled it; like as a child
in front of *The Equatorial Jungle*

that bearded cat; that bewildered owl?
monkeys & tea rose and grapefruit
picket fences, crowns or curated

tribal headgear, tiki bar
at the footlights & over
from the pipe cleaner

the closer to the equator the hotter
I heard, more or less
& it was a schema that made sense

& applied to you for instance
I would have stopped before
heading into: the jungle of you

until my fork hits bottom, a patch
of grey beige compostable, past
the spinach romaine arugula

cucumber endive chive. Spring
onion artichoke honeydew lima
olive tabbouleh quinoa

madness & someone has left
The Wall Street Journal.

II.

You As Invitation

Don't wash a wound with blood
Rumi says, and so, contra Rumi
I hoped we'd make it to that June wedding
RSVP on the table and
often I wake up as you're shambling
away, loping, disheveled, we're
a bit silly you said; no, I said
we're grounded; flat on our faces
on the ground, you said, is that
what you mean? I was some lower
phylum, reaction only

although I looked more like a fender
bender or rotten banana. They
were all more alive than we were. You
knew that June wedding was
another thing we'd never make.
Like the tomorrow restaurant
with tables in the water, I

harbored certain fantasies, so
that day in June I stopped by Harry's
you were there; one of your
absurd shirts, playing poker
with polka dots? Couldn't find
my suit, you said. Ha. What suit?
Rain on tin. Road swirling brown.
Spokes crushed and I knew
people must fight for what they've loved
and believed in even when it looks hopeless.

You As Hands

The drugstore where you bought the wine
twist top like a gas cap, and wading pool edges
wrapped in plastic and told yourself
those finger people in your head
think you're drinking juice, right?
Or, which rule? That doesn't apply to me.
They never do, but I know you mean
there are circumstances here
in other words: we are talking about: me

while the plot the man in the lobby
(I don't listen); the one thing after another
is always the same; what I notice
his knuckles under lines
like rain on the way to a drugstore
and after all as he continues, think how
I held yours up that time; grey
how it was too much for you to wash them
how it was too much for me to notice.

You As The Full Catastrophe

With black steam mold rising
elephant toes dark roots and luck
is a thing plucked from nowhere like
the mattress is thin and the pillow thick
post explosion foam rubber
fan hanging on by the sinews
and there's even a shabby pink bedspread

with checks, and the corroded TV
padlocked and chained and padlocked
no one would steal it but it might break out
scamper off? across the road? get on a bus?

I am just passing through like
the cold shower and ambivalent door
and wonder, how here I can live like

beyond the bars crazed
arachnoid eyeing the broken
louvers water tank trash bucket
pipe hose rag rope. Chicken wire
wheelbarrow rebar and how
(this keeps teaching me how)
here I can live, like

that day, you said, an epiphany:
it's all going to work out.

Fresh shirt and another in a grocery bag
what? Almost everything
matters less than you think.

You As Invasive Exotic

Bloated coral with shark eyes
bulldog head and sea lion crest
with whiskers, they call them barbels

and I think, meathead carp
slamming weights and bulging carotids
mealy mouthed carp. Pectoral
fin fans and tail arrows

missile carp
the way they can
bookend turn
and the pebbles underneath
how you can see them

and the outlines of organs
how you can see them
gecko carp
dark continents and
wavy trunk lines
smeared post paintball

carp, lipstick lady
with shopping trolley
will get to the parking place
first; carp-u-lence

and if they were
to come to a drop
like the ends of the earth

would plunge into the plunge
with the force of my (peer-

less) devotion, when I see you

drunk, and you haul me in
carp-e-diem:
you will remember
none of this tomorrow.

You As Sharp Object

back in the town in which
you are, undead
in the window, my reflection

same as that last day
T-shirt with pink spears
you said, and between windows

took you to tell me
those slices of pie
are spikes
and I remember
the half of it and you

are more than unlikely
to remember the other

all your stuff!
I threw it out!

But when I went back
only your kitchen
knife on the stoop.

You As Wreath

on the grass a sign for infinity
where men pull down
what they put up, a marquee
and how the wild horse says
he strangled me and how does it get like this?

The wreath is unbelievable.

Do you know what I mean when I say
unbelievable? *Gotta keep
a sense of humor right?* The reason
the wreath is unbelievable

it has just rained
the whites fascia
the reds jelly
donut, raspberry

pastry, carnations. With daffodil
fern, hammers and flames.
She is on fire with this
and I understand she will go back.
I am part jealous, I know
there's nothing like being loved that much.

The wreath is a hush
do you know what I mean by a hush?
I mean whipped cream bow
and silk snake trailing

like you're at a dinner party and you say
something they don't understand
maybe they are too clever, or the talk
is of philosophers and dirty jokes.

You As Teeth

Ghost dog, barrel ribs and belly
some worm, some parasite
eating her and you said, tourists
they like to get upset about it

and I nodded because we
understood: this is what's

so great about us: we know
the brutal nature of how it goes
because every day do you understand
we walk past one corpse or another.

The rooster? He's in a doorway
and thin as the dog. Two weeks
it took him to get from the garden chairs
to there and part pelican; crane says last
she saw him on a gurney and he's gone since
and it was you who told me, the drunks
they take them to the river.

Amaranth and dust coated *barbacoa*
I watch her eat and see your teeth
gutter yellow upturned party
some shindig and no one cared
what it would be like after; we never
clean up it's true but still, how
did they get like this? No one knows
and it's not interesting to anyone else.

Last time I saw you carrying
a block of ice, but I leeched
those thirty seconds already, dry.

You As Bathroom Essential

with beveled edges like the bench
on which we sat while I watched
our hopes and dreams as old leaf
snag on the banks of the River Cuale
while the woman washed her clothes
like I once did, and when my hands
dove into the foam, I saw them as severed
was this how I knew I was: home:
unpacking the soap like opening a tamale
it was so familiar as to be

(honeysuckle and beeswax
fat lye glycerine
tetrabutyl ethylene
and White Pigment number 6
CoffeeMate: vanilla) and yes

you can step in the same river twice
including the *atole* Cuale
which means (turbidity)
how much water so you can't see (us)
behind it? waxy your features, or

I thought I was looking at you but I wasn't
and is this why, can't stop inhaling you:
the morning tremor and your/my solution.

You As Crop Staple

More than corn to fix this
and even with butter powder cheese
and chili, as though it were that kind of
hunger. *Malecón*: barrels plate glass
and plastic champagne rows

bay and sky and the rusted prongs
of standing on end; I like to watch them

pile the cups but to eat I prefer the cob:
it speaks to my hunger to tear
at the kernels with my teeth
to pick the cylinder field clean

while Felipe tries to sell me something
scuba diving hang gliding
bracelets tequila pipes. *Terreno?*
Yes, a lot, he says, when all else has
failed; this last ditch attempt, to throw in

of course, but imagine when hunger strikes
and you are on your own lot.
After all you didn't buy it
because you wanted it to stay how it was.
I am happy enough with this *e-lot(e)*
I tell him, although I am not
as the pigeons swoop down
shard in my eyes like *jalapeño*:
the pitch ditch; what now?
When I am hungry, who will feed me?

You As Apples

I purple this moon
in the pulp
auditorium
ball and socket
fit like oversize
undersize
while you say
you built the house
or had it, lost, easy
come, I will die
in the same place
meaning you do &
that will something.

You As Barn Owl

and I mean how I could as soon penetrate
your miter, cassock and fascia

lagoon eyes chalk bluffs
and artichoke heart; your golden brew

stucco tattoo; champagne: you
in the glass, in front and behind

those friends in your grand stories
they're all dead, and you got me

on the way out, you say:
a shame. But I know

you have been dying much longer
than you say. One night you swooped down

velvet winged and in the tamale night
I wanted to be grasped in your beak

and lifted away by your four toed feet.

You As Weight

Cradling the keys for two padlocks
and how I'll remember to zip the pocket
so they won't drop out and how
this is the way I live, vigilant
and how, otherwise who will catch me
in my falling, and re vigilant:
who will catch you; me?

There is no more room on this boat
and it won't take on any more of that:
weight. We will both be in that way submerged
in that way coffin like in that way stones
in this field where we have come to watch
the large deaths of small creatures
goaded to fight and bleed discount red
and brutality, we can say, we know it

as you, from behind the parked cars
hitching your trousers, skinny as fuck
but face like Christmas morning

shaking the box, knowing what's in it yet
not daring to hope yet, not able to
contain the iridescent surface of it
on top of all that: weight.

You As The Rooster

Offer you *maíz* but you only want to
tell me how you got scooped up in El Tuito
or jumped in the parking lot behind the Pemex
and you'll be gone by tomorrow
all the way to Brownsville but I can see
the black on your fingers, the amber in your eyes
and where you slept, the doorway
the alley or the bridge or did
some stranger let you stay the night
and what did you have to do

answers create more questions
and I don't want to start this
it will be clear as head over heels
(backing away because no way no how
only one you even if you are everyone)

coxcomb sunset I tell you the day
has been the rush of a poster on a train
there wasn't only blurred content
just it was too fast for us to catch.

You As Cockfight

I.

The Rooster he's been going since a kid
a rooster at a cockfight, well, sure
but not fighting tonight at least not more
than usual, and like he was
with the bus driver to explain, *los gallos!*
Moon eyes while on the highway
hot lights and gravel fumes when he takes my hand
what else can I do but fly with him?
dizzying how the who is holding onto the who
we are like children playing chicken
with the zigzagging trucks and stumbling
into the ditch, we can only feel
how far down, but like with you, hand in
what else of consequence can happen.

Burning field, blanket covered
boxes lined up in the dust like stoves

II.

and this Rooster, his dad dead or in jail
the tenor of a memory and I search for clues
we are both detectives in this way
sniffing around the crime scenes of our lives

III.

what ranch is it from has it got scars
been stitched up, this means
and if you doubt between
the yellow and the red
go for the red, just odds
and it isn't always the bigger

sometimes the skinnier is quicker
and you cannot bet on the most beautiful bird.

Thousands of pesos, Rooster says
I won for José in Mismaloya
end of the night
he threw me a hundred.

IV.

Grasping them by the tail
they run them at each other
they push them at each other
they pull them back
away from each other

pushing and pulling
teaser bird

V.

and hold them like babies
while to tie on the knives
to stroke their feathers, whisper
then tug their throats
growl, slap and pluck

or they will do nothing
but be yellow and red but
unbloodied, dust scratching
under fluorescent tubes

VI.

propeller and cartwheel
collision and Rooster

demonstrates

a finger across the throat
light as foil, tender rooster neck

VII.

as the handler raises
stained glass to his lips
blood onto sand

arms outstretched

but death is already choking
on its blood; bubbling
hovering, slack
it hangs onto: nothing
while broken neck stuck
while half the crowd tastes

a won bet, the other a lost

VIII.

before it goes
beak to dirt
in the way of
the slowly then the
quick, under fierce light
in this little ring near *Las Juntas*
there is no more
of this, life left

amid the shouts
and money collecting

the hookers and lottery girls

weave around; children play.
And Rooster has brought more drinks.

You As Bottle

and I mean that other empty
bowler hat shouldered with
dust trails tin canned
from a fender, just married

crashed and gone insane
before the parking lot
the two headed eagle roadkill
flat against the glass

diamond quality, extreme purity

you do not do, anymore
after you said I'll marry you

get you a toy ring from OXXO

40 % Alc. Vol.
CONT NET 1L.

III.

You As Feral Cat

So maybe a bear can't be a lion
but there's no reason he can't
be a feral cat, for example
that one next to the rusted pipe

decanter neck and head blooms out
all round expectation.
Arrowhead ears, pampas grass
whiskers and handlebar mustache

all silly gringo waiting for the draw
holster flash and then the squander, silver
satin bib and colobus monkey tail

tucked in front like a sash
all silly gringo; all princess
with the cobblestones as cushions.

You As The Kitten

I found on the stoop
brought in then regretted it
not only did you rip up my purse
but I knew you liked you better than me

and often you said you were the kitten
playing with me; the herky jerk
and the rest, and it wasn't something
you did by halves

but plunged, fully, into

but a joke you said; look at you dopey
you're lucky I like dopey
come here, come closer
dance with me in the street
kittens in the street.

You As Small Space

Illinois behind the plates
everyone will have a back
and forward and forward and back
and to final up before the head

shake and this one on the palm out
to stop like; the reeling like, pavement like
climbing in your boat I was

trying to keep how much forward
I was trying to let how much back. Full

of the empty of closer-
(ness), even as you said
even though there is no
stone against room.

You As Paper Cup

with ouroboros slip to lid
on and while thinking

some again thing, some off thing
inside the bubbles

and coffee grinds are seam
to the drawn, a deserted

buffet or pillaged assembly
line with floors, roof, wall

and categories like syrup
for windows, shots, extras.

You As Canyon

Along the river that drop with no railing
and think how there are so many of them
balconies without bannisters
and footpaths along precipices
and holes in the street; from that point of view
not a safe place to be drunk
which is why we all are
on cobblestones and steps with crumbling
tongues: remember: your fear
of such things made me fearless
because I wanted to show you the world
is not as frightening as you think
I wanted to demonstrate
not the precipice, but the gorge

which means: we do not stumble
but plunge fully into

what is right there, muted; the bear park
(I saw its lights) and knew it was you
because I needed to know it wasn't
that other guy (the one with your shirt)
you have many fake twins:
the pizza delivery, tequila
salesman canopy tour, guy?

Best walk on the road; the gravel
from passing trucks is real as shard
sparking over the edge
disappearing into you.

You As The Mango

I picked off the ground
sea cucumber and uneasy
interior shifting. Yet
I knew you were not
overripe and that your
vial orange
would taste fine too

just a nudge against
the cheeks and tingle
being that close to gone.

You As Squirrel

When I mean how you
grasp the next straw
as that one goes

curl, rock, haul
squirrel chin ups:

your story of climbing into
that third story kitchen aside

you were younger and hungry
and it's only corroborated
by yet another, mad rodent

or: to squirrel things away
then come on with so much of it
next day, and speaking of layers
what it takes to make them visible.

You As White Rabbit

You see the raised down
between its black wall eyes.
This fishy déjà vu

like a hat trick
necromancy how I must have
called you to this hillside

of dirt and stones and tell me
the truth, now, your banana
leaf ears? Your horsey

prancing? Persimmon nose
and crutch walk? You tell me
your babies are kits, and a group

a herd; I thought it was a trace
how you hold out your paws
(no luck) it's worse today

the losing, feeling, more
faster. What battle, what fight?
You see. I would have

played that bad hand
which is another way
of being in a hat

or rolling it out, in spades:
the forgetting, sure, but
the remembering. How

I followed you down that
hole and then still asked
what? Wonderland?

IV.

You As Sea Urchin

bottom feeder and bottom dweller
you were not interested in the surface
you were all surface, even as rusted anchor

corrosion: *where two unlike objects meet*

she means a water tank
and a page thirty-nine
stuck on it, as I am on your spines

or picturing you at your wedding
(*they're not going to show!*
if you hadn't waited that extra minute.)

or leaning back to peel the card edge
(and only look once
you can remember two cards, right?)

or how you tell me your feet can breathe
smashed clubs, on the glass

in front of which I am
kneeling; a kind of atonement

and confessional:
sometimes you walk on your teeth

You As Snake

to wonder that leaf rustle and think
sliding over that wall you would
cut yourself on the blades, while
remembering how, as a child, afraid
of new, dark places and I try
to find this fear but like the train
you're expecting out the mountain
when what you don't know
the gleam is just imagination
always the glass was this thick with us

and what I'd give to be your beer
and cigarette bearer another
sun blanched morning along *Madero*
returning to you and since I can't summon
any fear of bogeymen and monsters
so; the concrete between cobblestone
is moving, so; ignoring warning sign(s)
like cardiomyopathy fatty liver
hepatitis, the look on your face
you said you look four.

and where did you go who did you see
and why did it take so long? I loved it
I knew it meant you cared

come here goofy; come here four
let me tell you what a whore you are
you're crazy, you're a whore, you're four.

You As Me In The Mirror

how in my pink and black 04
& when I use the hairdryer
I turn off all the lights (this

made you laugh): a sports team
that never existed; the memory of

as, you, who & it's true
I've never seen a whale
why would I when
I can look to your hills
flushing in the late afternoon

like I did then; it wasn't hot air
how you said, the sound of my fist
on your cheek, I never knew
how happy I could be.

You As Francis Bacon, *Figure With Meat*

Because you are grey? Because you are blue?
Because you have one eye? Or
because you are your face, screaming
in front of carcasses like slippers
to go with your mad pope robe
or elephant ears to match your rage
in this, your echo chamber, Xanadu
or a cardboard box; the idea of light beyond
but you can't see that and I can't
know that, and there is nothing either of us
can do with a white arrow on the floor.
Mouth like a strangling and I do not know
if you are alive or dead and still ranting
one hand grasping your cane.

You As Drag

the rip at the arm a moment of starfish
and sea horse before the first step, hip clash

fang sink or cruel *guitarrón*
I am a seminude ascending a staircase
my free hand going to ground

although this is already a bottom
I am searching for another
more usable, kind
but what there is; more red
agate and ballooning Bismark palm
B. nobilis and the intercostals
hold on as long as perforated paper.
Rolling on the bandage, a ribbon.
The trinket clasp with facing teeth.
Being swept off my feet.

You As More Red

(and it was mine I never saw yours, flow
like the River Cuale, rainy season)
or even creep, like taking a pulse or
wanting evidence, or, how the waiter
webs the tray, underneath

and when you rounded the corner
I looked up through the bougainvillea

and when you had my face
in your hands, an overcast day

and what to do but smash it
wall eave lantern boat tinman
Don Quixote; terracotta eye
storm and even with that washed out

what; you? Crimson ravines
and *achiote* Sierra Madres
look we have created worlds together.

You As Levels

looking for a picture of a wall
of course I came across: you
in your most immanent
young you but with familiar
eyes like a fish tank or measuring cup

and I was a gauger of levels
(considered myself an expert)
when the dashboard already said, you
are going too fast, like your dream
and I said, I think that's the pot

calling the kettle black, when how it went
gauged by the sheets and towels
and pillow cases, but still
I carried the tray with foil
and bag of *salsa roja*, back

to you; the tacos they were *machaca*
which of course you said meant crushed.

You As Slots-A-Fun

And I mean the way uppers
and downers, sure, but as lever
button or flip top
circus circus
tossed about by your bear paws
oven mitts
as I hand you
your drink with straw
(*hacer el oso*)
things will be different this time.

You As Tunnel

The night is drunk and walking home without you
so I have to, too. Past the tin can crack can
mold and Lemon Pledge and I'm back, dark
hallway of the villa not much by the sea where I lay
broken but in Technicolor following the script
whereby I will never mention what happened.

I am so close to you. You have done what I wanted.
I am so far from you. Look what you've done.

Flesh and bone we left me in that corner
next to the grocery bag under the painted window
on the green chair. I wait for you to pick me up

like a mop or dirty bed sheet, your awesome
disregard in the hot light it's nothing
to me what's everything, listen to you snore
(look how much you have loved me).

You As White Wall

(when I try to understand what
I'm tracking my hands along
no entry or exit to the stucco
& although the this then that
is semipermeable)

(& there is paint roller in that, like
the one dropped from your roof, or
how before you are all mouth
and spirit bear roar)

the rest is render what to think
of you what to make of you

(no go white wall go
stay white wall, come)

You As Cold Turkey

Cracidae, or the copper *chachalaca*
outside my window a rusty rig
engine sputtering or fucked up axle
with eyes like a nightmare aftermath

come let's be married in Vegas, sure
but what will we do for a ring?

Under the light of the moon my head
cracked on the tiles like an egg
you said, that time, at least I was out

but now every church bell every
chachalaca horn and release of cannons
the turkey who lives on the hill
chopsticks squabbling down stairs
I am cold; lizard face; lizard brain:
where was our pig? The chachalaca

builds its nest in March and April
which means there are chicks now, so why
are you still screaming? I knew I loved you
because I hurt you the most.

You As Yellow & Blue

like your kitchen, *talavera*: my perch
your boat and I am sweating, ice, I tell you

here it rushes from the fridge in cubes
(not like you, hacked from a block)

as the fifteen-year-old who comes to help
me into the bath: scraggly, mottled

fucked, like the tiles I am,
skittering, & who says, this isn't

what thirty-six looks like
the tumblers with yellow rim

(yours: blue) just as much
difference between the sky & the sea.

You As Corpse

and to cut to the chase is to find you, dead
in Xanadu and when I say dead I mean freshly
and when I say freshly I mean like a lagoon
and when I say stomach it I mean

it would smell like your month old dishes
in September; the spongy mishmash
firewheeling mold and jumblecloth
red, carp mouth, crocodile tongue

the pallor of the fridge like a dog, wailing
of course in death you are open at the heart

where the land crabs have come to feast
the white worm and gnat.

You As Puppy Killer

You watched it sink to the bottom
then dove in to get it

it turned skeleton in your hands
bone, ash, dust.

I thought, that's right
my blood is on your hands

but there was no blood
just bone, ash, dust

& the spider glove
I said that's your sickness

what you: rabbit pawed: held up.
I said spiders are symbols

even metaphors
you said they're just spiders

bone, ash, dust
& I said spiders don't have

bones & you said
shell, ash, dust.

V.

You As The Sun

while eggs milk butter sugar
boil on the stove then invert; flan

caramelization is
a doing what I will what

while you are honeycomb sweating
and eating beads, or *tacos adobada*

and the marination in time
for tourist season translated, meat.

You As Botanical Gardens

I. *Vanilla planifolia*

To go south is to be on the road to Xanadu
is to remember how I thought that new
OXXO, yes I should have been
consulted, and now there's a Subway too
(the same but different): talking to
the wild horse, I miss the hill
I used to climb, hand touching ground
to return to you and when I arrived
of course it was worth almost dying for
or, let me rephrase; you:

were mostly bear raging
and telling me what I was
to start with; I climbed to hear it after all
to take it in like stitching
epiphyte, one footed or

II. *Opuntia*

gleaming bats joint like
but easy separation
or how my head came apart

III. *Cosmos bipinnatus*

but we would rather peer into
the face of the Mexican aster
the tufted pink suns

while I think of vodka
cranberry, triple sec.
One foot falling into the cracks
like we have fallen into

IV. *Bougainvillea Glabra*

to articulate it; their magenta
leaves or flowers? seem
to be one then the other
masquerading as each other
or themselves, as we were
with trumpets, bassoons and

V. *Orchidaceae*

shark's teeth, chandelier
spaceships or how there
were no jelly beans and
what I'd give for a handful of jelly beans
right now the wild horse cries

VI. *Cactaceae*

while stopping to help the poplar with
its shedding like you once did
and shake it, leaning back
then move on like the organ pipe
rests against it as though it would grow right through
but even a succulent will not, having
started to go one way, keep on goading
the same, impossible

VII. Lunch

eggs with marigold yolks
jícama, lime and chili
while the *caciques*; banana
papaya, *mamey*, shrapnel and sparks
jaguar lilies with antlers
and hanging glass hearts

VIII. Fish

spaniel's ear folded
cochlear structure and when
I am watching a butterfly
I am watching a butterfly
(there is nothing else I am doing)

an odd lie gushing out like
from a burst pipe: mesquite and palm
how you looked into the empty pool
is not how I look into this brook:

when I make that pebble an eye
that current, a body
the scales the sun the quartz veins
snakeskin and crocodile

IX. *Bignoniaceae*

because if I've brought you up
once, I've brought you up
so I do not miss that hill

this time: to find
how the trumpet vines
have spilled over the road, making
it tunnel like but quaint, less
a portal into our glorious hell
than a picturesque entrance
way, side street: *callejón.*

You As The Toad

I chased around the apartment
with a poster roll.

You paused at the door

while I turned on the lights
inviting you go toad, go
back to where it's still dark

toad on a plank, won't jump

and how you are all parotoid
neurotoxin and breathing

through your skin (what
to think of you, what
to make of you) no go toad

go, stay toad, come.

You As Sound

and this is the subsequence
if I'm sitting in the sun
if I'm sitting next to the garden wall
in the sun if I'm sitting in a white
garden chair in the sun
and he's started singing
egg yolk orange and pumpkin
a sound to swim through
I can almost forget the staccato, remembering
how you were more often a legato
that's right, a slurred performance.

You As *Pied-à-terre*

and you've got said you funny
banisters, wires, missing
smashed cart and trash, hot dog

I compared it to a bomb blast
but *meant nothing negative*

I saw us there; on the laundry
I was drinking roof
and you were hanging cocktails.

You As *Salsa Casera*

flash of a rooster's (not beak, but)
tail; that rainbowing out, or the mosaic

labyrinth you followed, detoxing in jail
(that blizzard in the tropics)
the sting of chili, the hat tip of lime
cilantro spur, onion, tomato; *salsa*

a dance and a food to some people
the same thing although I
wasn't brought up that way
(we don't dance where I'm from
and we don't sing; don't ask)

but here I feel it as ectoplasm
or, today you are nourisher
not destroyer, and the garden chairs:

you on the red me on the green
white flag in between.

VI.

You As Leaves

As in fall red as in pale
as in buckets. As in a beach

theme remember as in
molasses as in imagine

the top layer of gravel, sliding
over the ground below

taking you, and hell no
you are not going to a doctor

and if I hadn't gone to Manzanillo
you wouldn't have been on that hill

and when they say let's pause
to consider the suffering in and out

do you know, if I turn I see you
hauling over a chair, aiming

as I do, for the safety of the corner
but it's times like these

we are trains leaping to another track
we do not know anything of the other route

but that doesn't mean it never happened.

You As Fierce Inhabitant Of Brackish Water

in the presence of decay makes
me think of your teeth and did you know I once
wanted to be a naturalist? And you
I asked, but your (sliding) answer didn't
satisfy; what do crocodiles want?

Extinction events: your talk of all the people
who've died, your infernal last man crawling
a bite stronger than a shark, stronger by far
than a bear. Sluggish but when propelled
by the force of your peerless, surprise, like me

you can stomach stones: beyond your jeweled
hide, wattle bask and rivet, your grey
gradient, in the way of the slow then the quick
and ex cathedra ping pong ball eyed joker

(so I'd know you were serious)
your ferocious life goes like that.
(A slip then the surface as before.)

You As Green Lagoon

And the ocean you can see it but only
go there, during times of flood like
dinner by the beach; *why not!*

on *Olas Altas* as you danced
algae and verdigris and nuclear crack up
growing a second head, green

and where I'm from (remember; don't ask)
a little lean on, depletionism

like your cove with tire scraps
beer bottles and drag marks
mental lakes are not even brackish

still I want to know what you don't remember
as though we could pin down, for example
how many memories to qualify

green as you are after all this time
it's too difficult to tie my shoelaces and green

you were a color belonged to someone else.
So, now, has this been devotion

to turn everything to you? Or
I cannot give it up, it's me it's mine.
Your green my green you're green my green.

Acknowledgements

Many thanks to the editors of these wonderful publications in which poems from this book appeared:

> kill author
A cappella Zoo
A-Minor
Anemone Sidecar
Bluestem
decomP
DIAGRAM
IthacaLit
Liberty's Vigil: The Occupy Anthology
NAP
PANK
qarrtsiluni
Referential
The Scrambler
Sea Stories
Used Furniture Review
Willows Wept Review

About The Author

Rose Hunter is the author of *[four paths]* (Texture Press 2012), *to the river* (Artistically Declined Press 2010), and *A Foal Poem* (2011). She is from Australia originally, lived in Canada for many years and then Puerto Vallarta, Mexico, where these poems were written. She now lives in Mexico City.